AF255215

Every Moment Is Now

Every Moment Is Now

A Poetry Collection

THOMAS JUAREZ

RESOURCE *Publications* · Eugene, Oregon

EVERY MOMENT IS NOW
A Poetry Collection

Resource Publications
An Imprint of Wipf and Stock Publishers
199 W. 8th Ave., Suite 3
Eugene, OR 97401

www.wipfandstock.com

PAPERBACK ISBN: 978-1-6667-6265-5
HARDCOVER ISBN: 978-1-6667-6266-2
EBOOK ISBN: 978-1-6667-6267-9

01/03/23

Contents

Contents

Acknowledgments

I would like to take this chance to thank Cameron University's Department of English and Foreign Languages, particularly the English Professors. The four years spent under their tutelage were both developmental and enjoyable. I feel as though it would be impossible to thank any one faculty member without mention of another, so I extend my profound thanks to each and every one of them.

I would also like to thank Wendy Dunmeyer for her advice, professionalism, and friendship.

A special thank you goes to Amber Byers of Tadpole Press for inspiring me to chase my dreams and for believing in me.

No thank you page could ever be complete without mention of my wife, Lucinda. I love you more than words can say.

Introduction

In an attempt to seek more balance in my life, I thought it might be a good idea to give meditation a try. Cutting straight to the chase, I was able to attend online meditations and speak with resident monks. I was amazed at how attentive the monks were to my line of questioning and at how kind they were while sharing their thoughts.

What I view as the most meaningful of our conversations centered around what many of us often refer to as living in the now. So many of us speak so openly about what it means to be focused on the now, but I felt the need to dig deeper. It seems as if I was in the right place because the very conversation that I needed was already beginning to reveal itself. The monk explained how each moment was its own moment and then went on to demonstrate how we could treat any moment as a new beginning, should we so choose.

By the end of our conversation, I remember asking him if I could be so bold as to make a statement akin to *Every Moment is Now.* No sooner had the words left my lips than I found my emotions welling up inside of me. I placed my hand over my heart, allowing the beauty of the moment to sink in. The monk remained silent, a sort of confirmational smile set in as I believe he sensed that I'd found what I was looking for.

Sounds too good to be true, I know, but I stumbled upon exactly what I needed and exactly when I needed it. You see, in the weeks leading up to our conversation, I'd been busy assembling a poetry collection. The collection was in need of a worthy title, one that supported its mode of delivery, one that boasted the fact that the collection does not restrict itself to a singular theme. Life does not work this way, so neither should my writing.

Each and every poem serves as its own moment, and every moment is now.

AUTUMN RAIN

A painting in your home's entryway has piqued
my curiosity, brother. While I cannot see their faces,
the ladies of paint hold lavish umbrellas to deflect rays
of sunshine from raining down on them. Here, the sun

greets an old raven as it sits atop a scarecrow meant to drive
him away. He picks insects from straw arms while squawking
at the familiar-looking face. Might he be reminiscing of days
gone by and of loved ones lost? The frightened man listens

while he watches that old hound dog of yours. He was over
there, lazily lapping up sunshine until a few short moments ago.
That's when the silence began to strike and the hushing sounds
of rainfall began approaching from dark skies in the west.

The onset of mild depression brought about by autumn rain
soothes my inner child. It brings back memories of sipping the
hot butterscotch apple cider our mother made. She'd fog the
window as she whispered rain is to sunshine as teardrops to smiles,

And do you remember, brother, the child seated in the mud puddle?
She was crying and alone. Heartbroken over a loss I can no
longer remember, yet I remember her, and the cold, pooling
waters in which she wept. The calm in your voice delivered a

sense of belonging to her injured, but otherwise beautiful heart.
She followed as we made exit from the rain and re-entered our

home. Do you remember, dear brother? That day was much like this. I'll grab the cider and you the towel. Bring in the hound.

CYCLICAL

Danger searches for purpose during the hours of darkness, so they sleep. Rolling pillows over in unison, humans in hardened structures instinctively crave cool surfaces for their warm bodies.

As the world around them fights for life, they rest. In one corner of the rounded planet, the yellowed teeth of a tiger puncture the mango-flavored flesh of a sambar deer, while in another corner,

a lioness celebrates the taste of gazelle and seeks out water. She cautiously approaches the edge, instinct reminds her that she is the prey in this place. One, two, three tongue taps of water and

she's safely on her way, sleeking past a busy spider reaping the rewards of a web well spun. Avoiding such obstacles as sound, day breaks the darkened clay clouds of the night, ushering in

light and heat from millions of miles away. From the tallest of all mountaintops to the lowest of earthly valleys, these gifts are harvested. Protective outer casings conceal silent, one-sided

battles as chlorophyll soldiers begin their march. Hot coals of light are escorted to their cells and imprisoned until spilling their truths and releasing their oxygen. Humans emerge from

their dwellings. They run, play, hunt, and forage, aware only of that which the eye can see. Plucking flowers for fragrance seems an odd method of appreciation but, whatever it takes. The world wobbles on its wayward axis and all that is living celebrates the struggle to remain that way, but the night bites back. The cooling might seem safe, but it's best to hide until the dawn— if you can.

SOULFUL SOUTHERN MORNING

Morning roars in.
Flickers hammer on trees
not more than a stone toss from my back door.
Had I been so inclined to sleep in on this brisk spring
morning, I would have missed their neighborly communique.

Fragrant offerings from mimosas and magnolias
make life worth living—

My father, God bless his soul,
always referred to grits as *southern ice cream*, and so,
I've made a habit of having this treat a mere six days out of seven.
Fried hard eggs on Bavarian rye reminds me of my mother.

Dear mother is undoubtedly sipping hot coffee
by the kitchen window at this very moment—

I slice thin slivers of the rye, then let the grits
simmer and the eggs fry. Like mom, I'm already
sipping the morning brew and, just like mom, I've already fed
the crows. So, I slap the eggs over the toast and ladle the steaming
hot grits into my favorite bowl with two thin bricks of butter.

The best is yet to come as nature's radiance calls to me
from outside my own kitchen window

OF PERSIMMONS AND PLUMS

I

I can still feel the crunch of dried leaves beneath my feet as if last
year were yesterday—

Time passes like molasses through my heart's hourglass
now that you're gone, but I can still remember your cheeks,
redder than rhubarb and lightly splashed over a silky white
backdrop. The artisan's woolen tarp is draped lazily over his
timeless treasure, and eyes green as emeralds.

Too cold, too soon. Leafless trees wore blankets of white to cushion
their tender persimmons—

Beneath your treasure of emeralds and tartly splashed
cheeks lie a wonderland of whetted tenderness. I could
only think of the satsuma plums dangling from their
branches in adjacent orchards, twice sprinkled with
cinnamon and once splashed with vanilla, then served
with just a dash of confection.

II

Our kyusu boiled over, spilling the fragrance of our love into the
goodness of the night—

III

When spring rains flooded the orchards, they carried you away
from me and my soul followed—

IV

Winter passes through the orchard once more, and once more I take
a crunch along the leaves—

Fog from my breath fills the evening air, surrounding your
sanctuary within my dreams. Back in this reality, I splinter
frozen wedges from still, mirrored currents before gathering
and stacking dried branches. Shreds of kindling are added for fuel.
Steel strikes flint causing friction. Fire needs air to breathe. And so

I breathe, inadvertently inhaling airborne coals and re-igniting
unknown remnants of my soul—

Combusting fires within my being are paralleled by colored
dreams. The red and yellow flames of a fiery dragon hiss at the
icy cold winds of a blue dragon. I can feel the magic as I fill the
clay teapot with persimmons, peppercorns, ginger, cinnamon
sticks,and ice wedges. It glows as it boils over hot coals.

Plated plums, sprinkled cinnamon, splashed vanilla, and confection—

accented by the tender fragrance of hot persimmon tea.

CARTRIDGE

Pieces of tomorrow scatter on the ground beneath my feet.
The choices I must make are not those of my choosing but
I must choose all the same. After an arduous life, my body
has been falling apart and so I make the only choice I can.

The soldier would proudly limp away from a uniform
that was just the right size but failed to fit him anymore.
With a salute, I accepted a folded symbol of my country's
freedom, in effect exchanging a known journey for the

unfamiliar road of shadows. For so many years, this was
the joke: don't become a casualty of your own dependence
to a lifestyle unsuited to bad knees, bad ankles, bad hips,
and a back that carried a nation's hope but can no longer carry

a rucksack. In truth, the limping away was the easy part when
compared to that one good ear and that one good eye, and the
pitiful need to hear someone ask for them to turn 'round. I know
these soldiers carry way too much pride to admit they'll miss me.

No longer a soldier, I am a citizen. No longer needed, I am a
second-class citizen to those who now guard my post. From
the highest office in the land to the private on the rifle range, I
have become the spent cartridge, slightly hidden beneath the

sands of forgotten service. Powder expended and payload delivered, I must be properly disposed of so that I may join my comrades in arms within buckets of permanence. My three volleys echo softly and my people remain free. Simply perfect.

BORDERS

I have built guarded borders of torment in an effort to protect
myself from emotion—

Much like a mason, I've built walls to anchor chains.
One chain will keep my hands from reaching out,
another will keep my feet from running away,
and the last will lock my lips so that I cannot ask for help.

My hands touch my face, and I feel so damn ugly.
I don't like to be touched when I'm like this and I
will not come to bed just now. I need to look into
my mind's reflection until the mirror cracks a smile.
Chain one.

Do you really believe I want to be this way?
Day after day I chased shadows into the darkness,
I chased happiness, and hope, and love. I know
my mind wanders, chaining my feet seems the answer.
Chain two.

Do not speak to me as if I were a child. Remember,
if I were intent on hurting myself, I would have done so
and had it over with. Please tell me you can see that.
My words betray me, and the world judges me harshly.
Chain three.

Light crosses over borders and warmth eases torment, but only love may loose these chains.

IN THE DARKNESS

Here, in the cold of the darkness, I distance myself
from the world. I want only to be with you, whatever
the price, with you. The night closes in around me as
darkened swaths of cold air thicken and greet me.

I back further into a corner of mirrored
walls, retreating from reflections of despair,
from the eyes behind the glass
and the teeth beneath the eyes.

Clouded moisture oozes, whetting the
appetite of the beasts behind the glass as
sudden bursts of warm air drive them back.
I know it's you, show yourself.

What is this you say? I should not have come. But—
my heart—it aches—it aches to be with you. If I must go,
then a kiss goes with me. Please, just one kiss, then I'll go.
I ready myself for the reward of your embrace

but your warmth passes through me
as if time through the never-ending
expanse of space. The eyes and teeth
from the mirror return as the stinging

bite of reality hits me like an axe
striking a grape. I know now, the terrible
truth from which I run. I know now,
beloved, which one of us slumbers.

PHOENIX

The journey to your dig site was a long one.
As I look over the once lush fields of One Life
Fossil Beds, I'm greeted by dirt mounds.

The dirt mounds cover the grasses which once
covered them, and pits dug by treasure hunters
decorate the landscape with deep, square polka dots.

On the defensive, you remind me that this is anything
but a treasure hunt, and that the very essence of what
makes us who we are possibly lies beneath our aching feet.

You continue to ramble on about the varied opinions of
where life began. Even the workers you've assembled here
are convinced that the meaning of their lives lies in wait.

At this very moment, I am inclined to offer a solution. Do
not continue this search for the meaning of life, my friend.
Instead, find a way to give your life meaning. But who am I

to judge your beliefs? So, I choose the role of the silent friend.
I find myself hoping that your phoenix will rise from the ashes
and that knowledge sought brings knowledge gained. Now dig.

SKIES OF BLUE LONELINESS

Chasing skies of blue loneliness,
    abandoning all thoughts resemblant of love.
I have chosen to dwell here.
    Despondent, devoid of all emotion save sorrow.
Hurry along now. Do not wait for me.
    I wish to be alone, so that I may weep, alone.

Hiking through mountains of solid rock, I spot a pebble.
    Single and solitary, the pebble lies alone.
Pausing through moments of eternity, the pebble and I immix—
    From a distance, from afar.
I halt my advance. Isolated, as am I, it must remain alone.
    Remain alone, remain safe.

Trudging through swamps of black waters—
    they appear lifeless, as does my soul.
Engulfed within dark, stale torrents. I search for isolation.
    It is that which I seek.
Expressionless—Emotionless—I am completely numb.
    Should ripple or wave fashion beaut, I will feel no pain.

When the sun rises over the easternmost boundaries of my depression,
I will journey west,

and so, I run   chasing my shadow   indeed, chasing tomorrow—
    Chasing skies of blue loneliness.

A RIDE THROUGH THE NIGHT

I ride,
and the steed on which I ride, changes as often as my mind, though
I have no mind.

Today,
my steed neighs, shaking the vast emptiness around me, reminding
me that I have been

circling a clouded, blue planet which I once
called home. It is a constant reminder of what it
means to be ordinary. Indeed, It is a constant reminder
of what it means to be grounded, and of what it means
to have skin, and flesh, and bone. All are gone, and

Today,
I am what earthly beings would consider to be celestial, yet I am
not Lord.

I ride,
and the blue mass which I have circled for the past year releases me,
enveloping me in stardust as

I re-imagine myself now, as a knight clad in armor. I imagine my
stallion to be equipped in much the same manner and I imagine
our path through the night of the day. On this path, I imagine each
moment grants a promise of rebirth, and another day just like this.

I ride,
and in this moment, I captain a porpoise, commanding every move
with my mighty trident, for—

Today,
I am set adrift upon the waves of celestial oceans, gliding over
dream-filled starfish. Ha—

folding space into origami figures is like time travel for

beginners. Tiny pockets of venture conceal themselves

between rogue folds but are easily avoided by remaining

centered on time. But time, it waits on no one, and none knows

time. For time is the metaphor and space, the immeasurable.

Today,
I passed the ice giant as if it were a pebble. Its frosty aura reminds
me of a previous life, yet

I ride,
tugging on the reins of my hydra. Veering left of the bright star at
the foot of the hunter,

passing safely into his core as my beast and I are sucked

into blue, and we are sucked into red. The history of

mankind hits me like a rainstorm. Lightning crackles and

thunder booms as a battered mass is granted mercy. The

inherent goodness of man warms my heart as, once again,

I ride,
slung from reflections of a species two steps from doom, and three
steps from greatness.

Today,
all that was wrong was made right, and all that was fractured was
mended.

As molecular clouds breathe me in and I, once again, am
bathing in pools of reflection: I am the seed within the womb.
Light beckons me forward as I claim the sentient being's
heartbeat. This was my life. My crawls, my walks, my falls,
my falling in love, and though I died, love remains, and

Today,
I emerge from my reflection, headed for absolution, headed for the
mighty beetle, so

I ride
atop a great horned beetle of my own making. Together, we are one.
Together, we are fierce.

But the hunter plucks me from the night and laughs as he
fashions my beetle into an arrow which he uses to taunt the
twins, teasing both Castor and Pollux with a meal they cannot
taste. Found by the hunter to be deserving, I am to be launched
through the expanse of the night. Into night to search for the day.

I ride
the arrow of the hunter through the night of the day. For, through
the eloquent darkness,

Today,
I see past the charioteer, to wheels which feed the night air, allowing
the fires of the kiln

belonging to the Goat Star to affix fresh souls to human
clay before blasting them through the night and to the
blue planet which I once called home, that place— so ordinary.
I feel goodness as a bright vessel whistles past me. May you be
forever brave, and may you be forever kind, but as for me,

Today,
I have landed so softly 'pon shores made from the petals of the cherry
blossom.

I ride
no more. Be this the beginning, or be this the end, I have arrived—home.

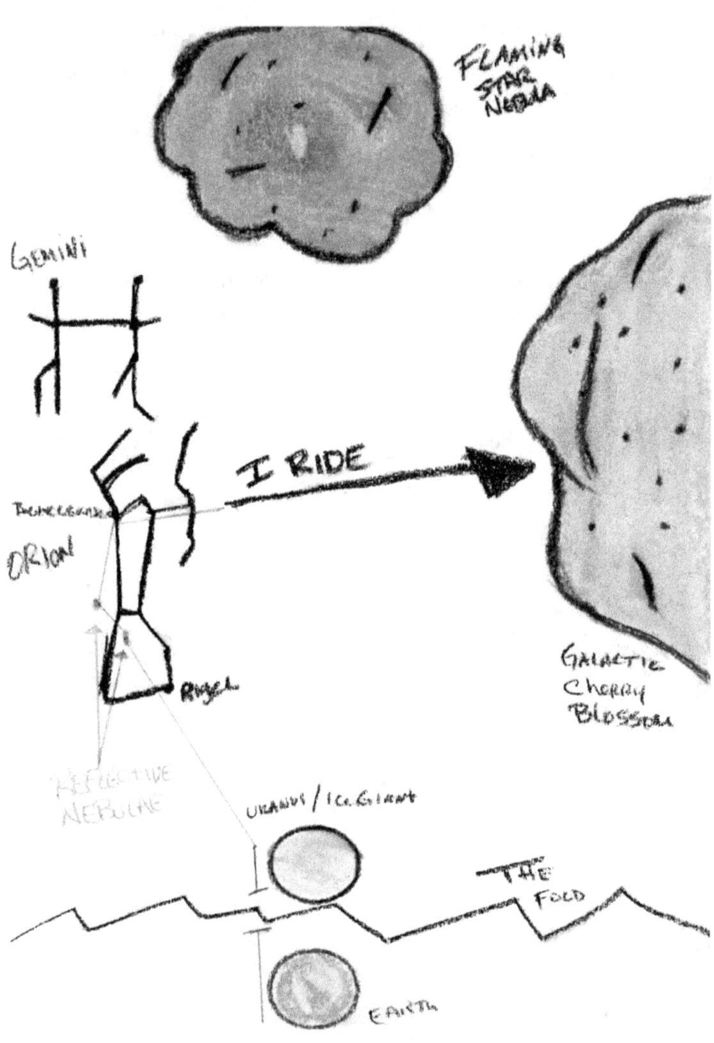

FLAMING STAR NEBULA
GEMINI
ORION
Betelgeuse
I RIDE
GALACTIC CHERRY BLOSSOM
Rigel
REFLECTIVE NEBULAE
URANUS / ICE GIANT
THE FOLD
EARTH

DARE TO REMEMBER

We are seated in a circle speaking of loneliness, yet we are here,
together—

When I think of loneliness, I'm reminded of Chilean desert
sands. Sands that stretch as far and as wide as the eye can see.
How then, could I have possibly found it so amusing to thrust
a rain gauge deep into the dry and coarse carpet cast over these
lands? I want to speak of this today and I want to tell the
isolated souls seated in this circle of my experiment. You see,

the thought process behind the placement of that metal and
glass measuring cup was to determine if the inanimate could
feel loneliness, as if a rain gauge had feelings. My friends and I
snorted and chuckled as we sat a fair distance away to record the
isolation we'd created. Winds moved in quickly and we were left
with no place to run, so we huddled together for safety while dust

devils collided into a full-blown sandstorm. From here, the world
was a brown blur for nearly an hour. When we were sure it was
over, and we could no longer detect the faintest of whistles, we
took inventory of fingers, toes, and their owners. Oceans of sand
made it difficult to regain our bearings, but a compass led us to the
rain gauge. There it was, full of sand and no longer alone. I want to

tell them of this for so many reasons, but I am afraid that they will
think me simple. Perhaps I am simple, but we cannot end loneliness
by searching for barriers to break down. This will not satisfy your

sense of being. Trust me, this is not relevance. The day we cast aside our umbrellas and frolic, carefree in the rain will be that day. I dare you, remember that which you are so eager to forget.

I dare you— remember—*you.*

CICADAS AND SYCAMORES

I woke, sunny side up and ready to roll into
a fine fall morning. Mother was already two
steps ahead of me, popping egg yolks and
allowing the perfection of emulsification
to spread itself across my morning toast.

Devouring my sammich and washing it down
with warm tap water, I grabbed a wedge of
sliced honeydew, dashed through the door, and
cleared the four steps beneath the patio, sticking
the landing, of course. I spotted your ponytails

as they pranced across the open field, and knew
exactly where you were headed; to the mudhole
we called a pond and toward another day living in
the fairy-tale world that you and I built, together.
Brick by imaginary brick were stacked without the

opinions of others. I knew that playing pattycakes
and baking mud pies wasn't exactly a favorite pas-
time of most boys at my age, but you were my girl,
and I was happy being whatever you wanted me to be.
That day, we found the skeletal remains of a cicada

clinging to the bark of an old sycamore tree that
we'd carved our initials into. I remember marveling
at how a bumbling mass of bug emerged from one

shell, before waiting on another to dry and harden.
Then I remember a tickling peck on the cheek and

the stern voice of your father that followed our
moment of childhood bliss. He nearly pulled your
arm clean off when he stole you away from me.
I snuck in a smile that evening by the ice cream
truck, but the old goat just wouldn't let it be. He

scolded you again and I watched warm torrents of
tears roll off your cheeks, melting the volcanic
surface of your ice cream cone. Lava flows of
melted ice cream were oozing over your fingertips
and there was nothing I could do. That was many

years ago, and now, as our young daughter sleeps
peacefully between us, I know exactly how your
old man felt that day. There simply must be a way
that I can protect her from the whole wide world.

MY CURSE

I've long thought it my curse, my constant failure
to openly express love. Almost as if I were that one
person in a million who lacked the ability to express
their emotions due mostly to the barriers they'd constructed.

My mind tells me both blessing and curse come from a very real
place, and that there are stained-glass passages leading to the heart.
Should light get trapped within the heart, then it will beat no longer.

But my heart tells me that the love I have longed for must be allowed to
travel through such passages, and that silhouettes of hope and happiness
are hidden purposefully within lightly colored layers of illumination.

For the answer, I must search my soul.
If we are truly the offspring of water,
then life-giving raindrops of wisdom
will lead me there.

It's pouring outside, and the
stained-glass windows between
my heart and my mind finally agree.
I love you.

NEVER BEEN HERE BEFORE

This place, it seems so familiar—
tell me, have I been here before?

Love, you say.
But there's no such place.

Love is a thought,
a dream,
a convenient reason to act the fool.

I've often heard of love being expressed as a who or a what, but
never a where—

I do remember taking a hard left at hello, and
then I remember walking through endless fields of irises,
all while staring intently into your eyes.

It's said there are more colors of the iris than the great Van Gogh
would know what to do with—

And to be honest,
I was looking through such a foggy filter, that
I couldn't distinguish one flower from the next.

I remember the reds and yellows of the fire,
I remember the white-hot heat of desire,
and the blue. Mostly, I remember the blue.

My internal compass spins like a clock out of time,
my heart follows you, with no reason and no rhyme.
Where are we? What place is this?

The more I see as I walk through the door, I do not believe I have
ever been here before.

NOTHING LEFT TO SAY

Where are you?

I thought we had a deal.

So, please—
    Call me.
    Text me.
    Tell me—
    Tell me anything.

I could feel something in the air that night—
    the night you left.

And now I'm left here, alone.
    You know—
like a lion who's been caged for too long.
    Yes, like that.
    Just like that.

I cannot help but wonder to myself, and—
    and sometimes,
    I wonder aloud.
How did it all go so wrong?

    Was it me?
    Was it you?

Does it—
Does it even really matter?

Every single time the phone rings, I panic.

I'm scared that I've lost you,
    and not just *for a while*.
I'm so scared that we've all lost you.

    I go from angry to sad,
    from sad to numb,
    eventually returning to anger.
    Perhaps being angry is what I do best.

When you get home, we'll play make-believe and act like nothing's
wrong—
    Until it happens again.
    Without a fuss.
    Without warning.
    Without—

    Without so much as a goodbye.

So, tell me,
where are you?

RED FROM ROSES

The rose petals feel so soft and smooth
as prickly stems invade my flesh, peeling
back layers of fibrous collagen. I'm happy
to see you still love me.

Salt from the ocean's breath effectuates a
blissful burn. Pain reminds me I'm alive
and a thick red teardrop bids me good day.
It tells me you still care.

I am so eager to touch you, so eager to
hold you, so eager to love you. The red
from the roses paints a target on my lips—
one kiss to wake me.

Each second without you has aged me a day.
After surviving five perceived centuries of
loneliness, the reward of two roses for two
days symbolizes your love.

Bitten by one, I send the other on a wave, like
one would a message in a bottle. In the morn,
when you leave again, a rose rides the seas with
you. As for tonight, please stay.

BEAUTIFUL

Before you say a word, my love, let me look into your
Eyes. Let me see through them, past them, and into
Another dimension. A dimension where the sun rests
Until the shadows dance and the moon tugs at my heart,
Teasing my emotions as they rise like the tide.
Is it so much that I ask of you? I want only to be your
Fool and to live my life in a manner which makes full
Use of every opportunity to please you. I beg of you,
Look upon me one more time, before you say a word.

MY FATHER'S SON

Mortality's stinging reminder is delivered
as if flown in by murder hornets from abroad.
A life well-lived is a life well-observed, so I watch
as theatrical characters act out memories I'd all
but forgotten. They come to me now, in dream.

These apparitions soothe my battered emotions
and offer advice from beyond the grave, which
they deliver in the voice of my fallen father:
Don't be a fool and waste away these precious
moments, son. They are forgotten in an instant.

Dreams, like flowers, you see, await sunshine and rain.
Or, maybe, in this dream, they await any soul
foolhardy enough to invest their precious time and effort.
But for what? Just to seize the day like the wisest of fools.
As I ponder this and more, I am reminded that I am also my

mother's son. She weeps, remembering the man she loved, the
man who loved her. He was the man who loved and raised her
children, he was the man they all wanted to be. The sunshine,
you see, has followed the rain, and in saying farewell we give
thanks to the man who gave everything, until the very end.

A DOG

I want to hear a poem about a dog. A dog like my dog.

A real sweet dog, like a tale of the tail, wagging on that
    beautiful tail dog.

A loyalty beyond compare dog whose eyes say *look what I found*
    when he's stealing my burger kind of dog.

A *My kingdom for a blanket* dog who won't move over to let me
    back under that blanket kind of dog.

The art of the bark kind of dog who says *hello* because everyone
    just looks so damn familiar kind of dog.

That's right, this is a poem about an *I'm digging holes in the yard
    because it smells like victory* kind of dog.

The nose knows is all about a dog, and my dog is a hound dog.
    In other words, his nose really does know.

A dog who knows who's the boss, like my dog. He's the boss,
    and what's more, he knows it. That kind of dog.

This dog saved my life, and I will be forever grateful. He is a dog
    that deserves much more than I could ever express on paper.

My dog is so much more than just a friend.

WAKING UP

This morning,
I woke up to crackling bones—
to sore joints and greyed hair.

How the hell did this happen?
I'm only—

Damn!

In my youth,
I was told that old age
would sneak up on me.

Liars!

The years,
They were not tiptoeing around in the kitchen,
Nor were they hiding behind closed doors.

I was young—
carefree—
at the very top of my game.

This morning,
I woke up old.

CHIN WHISKERS

I remember the man, the soldier, the tough guy.
The very man who's go to emotional response was anger,
whose sadness was an empty glass of bourbon.

I was the sort of stiff who believed that tenderness
could be achieved through the marinading and pulverizing
of a slab of meat. No longer can I be that man.

No longer can I deny myself the laugh, the smile, the hug, or the
kiss. No longer—

I rub my chin-whiskers and look at the little girl
in front of me. She smiles and laughs and melts my heart,
like a piece of candy that's been in the summer sun for too long.

I try my best to look away, but her warmth melts my heart again and
the candy grows softer—

At this very moment, I find myself wondering exactly how
my wife is going to feel, knowing that the chin-whiskers of
the old man have become as permanent as the smile on his face.

Relax, she'll be fine with it.

COLD BURNING COAL

Battening down the hatches and chasing away my dreams, I lie here
in wait—

Lightning strikes and shutters are blown open.
The cold winds of winter creep in and begin
rummaging through my hair as if looking for something.

There's nothing left but memories, I'm afraid. Memories of
a heart run on cold burning coal, memories of the love for
which I have craved since the moment you left.

Old man winter plucks a hair follicle. Is that where
my memories are stored? This hair follicle is thrust
into my eye so that I may see, and indeed I do.

I see the woman who once called my heart home,
And I see the woman who, upon leaving,
scornfully shattered every window in that home.

You wore red that day.
We cuddled and played
in the apple orchard, beneath the safety of trees.

Looking back, it was all too soon.
You were not willing; hence the kiss was stolen.
Both anger and blush redden the face. Initially, I believed it the latter.

As the red dress darkened, and as the red in your
face lit the fire in your eyes, the former revealed
the latter was false hope. Can you not forgive me?

From that day to this I have been alone, freezing from a heart run
on cold burning coal.

ICE COLD FUSION

I've grown old,
Cold with a lack of desire.
Every day I am without you

Casts a shadow
Over an otherwise
Lighted plane.
Do I mean enough

For you to turn around?
Unable to breathe, I
Suffocate.
I
Only
Need you to fuse my heart to my soul.

DREAMS

In my dreams, I am alone.
The desolate hunter
whose prey rests, unaware—

unaware of my presence,
unaware of my hunger,
and unaware of my needs.

As I pass, I inquire of the darkness:
what beautiful creature is this?

Touching all it sees,
smelling all that blooms,
and caressing all that lives.

In my dreams, we two are one.
I am the protector, and you, the protected.

Until we no longer feel the sun's rays.

Until we reach forever, and then, always.

HIGH ON A ROOFTOP

A man stands high on a rooftop in an attempt to feel alive.
The wind blows through his hair and the sun taps him on
the shoulder. He laughs at how small people look from here.

A bird nests high on a rooftop in an attempt to keep her little
hatchlings safe. The winds carry promise as breadcrumbs arrive.
Unconcerned with the onlooking man, she tends to her young.

A June bug lands high on a rooftop, they're such clumsy little
critters. Winds whipped the little bug and shimmied him up the
side of the building. He will be a fine dessert for the hatchlings.

Rescue crews arrive high on a rooftop in an attempt to sway the
man from jumping. The wind muffles his voice as he tells them
he is just fine. Strange how muffled just fine sounds like suicide.

A man steps off a ledge, his feet touch the surface high on a rooftop.
He says that he's ok before he's strapped, wrapped, and escorted
away; deemed crazier than a cuckoo, as the cuckoo tends her young.

A DAY SOAKING IN SUNSHINE

Rays from the sun strum upon strings of duality, soothing my soul with heaven-sent goodness.

Hidden within the goodness my body yearns for are tiny little demons, they turn goodness to despair.

Perhaps I'll just sit out here a while in hopes that good vanquishes evil. Just a while, for my happiness.

My hound dog, Louie is his name, he sniffs and scratches and pays me no mind. He scans, and searches.
Only he knows of the treasures beneath the soil, only he knows of that which he seeks. I watch, lovingly.
He's found something, a morsel, perhaps. Without hesitation or celebration, he's eaten it, whole.

As the hour grows late, retreating rays of sunshine project my shadow downward. I believe it dances.

I see now, why man chases shadow. In contrasting duality— I see, also, why man fears shadow.

Come now, Louie. You've eaten enough. Perhaps we'll soak the sunshine in again tomorrow, perhaps.

A COOL SPRING DAY AT THE ZOO

The gates are large, warm, and welcoming as if we were on safari,
but safe.

I see a red-headed man and a red-headed woman pushing a baby
buggy—Red-headed child.

Puppy dogs are being carried in purses and children are wearing
leashes. What gives?

We don't have any children with us but
we walk through the petting zoo all the same.
I guess we just love to see the goats and the
donkeys, but why do the wallabies always sleep?

A child's eyes get as big around as hockey pucks when they see
gorillas. Mine too—

The gorillas always seem to have offspring, and
their frolicsome nature makes them a joy to watch.
Oh, my goodness, the orangutan only has one eye!
Never mind, the other half of his face was covered.
Wait. All of the primates have blankets today.

You stop and smell the flowers despite your allergies (sneeze) God
Bless You—

I love the plants at the zoo because they're all so
perfectly lush. Now hush, bamboo means we're

entering the kingdom of large cats. The lion needs
a hairbrush, and the tigers need more space. The
jaguar looks as if its jaws were made of smelted
muscle. Ok, we've seen the fishing cat, we can go.

We stop and sit for the elephant show and a geriatric female obeys
commands for onions—

Asian elephants have ears that fit their face, while
the African variety have bigger ears that get all over
the place. Did you know that? After I've bored my
significant other with the same old facts as last year,
we move on to the modern-day dragon that is kept
behind glass. Whipping its forked tongue into the air,
he pauses before lifting his head and staring at you. I
told you not to wear perfume, but you just don't listen.

The day is getting longer and, in case you haven't noticed, so are my
stanzas—

You still won't come in and see the snakes with me but
that's your loss, not mine. The bears, the bison, and the
fish behind glass are all doing just fin, I mean fine. Do
you remember when that silly girl dropped her phone
right next to the alligator pit? The alligators were smiling.
I'm telling you; she almost fell for it. It's a good thing I
was there to save her. What? No! we're not leaving before
we see the giraffes; they are my absolute favorite. How is it
the blood travels up those long and spotted necks anyway?

Another great day at the zoo, and the animals were all just lovely.

TAKE MY HAND

Take my hand dear lady, the time has come
for one man and one woman to grab the world
like a grape, squeezing its goodness into wanton
lips and relishing the taste of something intended

to enrich our lives. For why else would nature have
gifted us the grape? What possible use could it carry
other than to open our minds to the possibility of
heaven, as if the heaven I have found in your embrace

wasn't proof enough. Dear lady, the clock's hands have
begun to quicken and there's not a moment to waste.
The world is awash with fools, intent on turning away
from the sunshine. More for us, I say, as we sow the

seeds of our love into lush and fertile soils. Moisture
from our lips whets the future of our bounty and grants
us the gift of laughter. Little feet widen our path and
brighten the sandy beaches which lie beyond our horizon.

Life is a teardrop filled with nectar, a rose petal floating
on air, an adventure that has yet to be defined. Love is a
blessing from one to another. Can you see the floating rose
petals as they weep with joy? They sweeten the grapes.

EVERYTHING FEELS LIKE ZEN

I take a deep breath and realize:
The air is not mine,
indeed, the air is me.

I take a good look all around me.
I can see everything,
and I am one with all I see.

I taste blue lights—
'tis the horizon.
It tastes of fruits, of spices, and of honey.

Teasing my palette,
the spice of life is sweeter
than the sweetest of honeycombs.

Like you and I,
this planet is alive. Listen as
it labors for every last breath.

Now, I smell a flower.
Inhaling its goodness.
The flower is me and I am the flower.

CRYING

Today, I saw the clouds cry.

I tell you,
puffy white pillows floated on air as I stared—
stared into your eyes as you stared into mine.
The sun would rise, and the moon would fall,
behind the eyes of clouds, and we saw nothing—
we saw nothing at all.

Today, I saw the sun dance.

I tell you,
heat from the heavens was on display as I prayed—
prayed for your warmth. We'd be free, you and me.
The rain would subside, as the clouds would displace,
horizons washed away, as the tears flowed down—
they flowed down your face.

Tonight, I saw the moon rejoice,

I tell you,
all the stars in the sky, they make a mess of the night—
but, as the night falls, it recalls the name being carried on the
wind. It is to be delivered by way of scented whisper. By way
of cool skies, lilac, and moonlight. How perfect for goodbyes.
Goodbye, baby. Goodbye.

TELL ME

Say I'm the one—
the one of your dreams
whenever it seems
like your heart's come undone.
Say I'm the one.

Tell me that you love me—
forever and for always,
for the rest of my days,
whenever that may be.
Tell me that you love me.

My passion grows stronger—
When push comes to shove
You're the one that I love.
No longer can I wander,
My passion grows stronger—

and I swear I'll be true—
until the sun sets behind
the brown of my eyes.
My love's just for you,
and I swear I'll be true.

THROUGH YOUR EYES

If I could see me through your eyes, I wonder
What would I see?
Would I see me?
Or would I see the me I think is me?
Perhaps I would see the me of your dreams.
But would that still be me?

If you could see yourself through my eyes, I wonder
Might you fall head over heels?
Could you tell me how it feels?
Or would you wonder if you're enough?
Perhaps you could see the dilemma I see
As I wonder out loud, *do you love me?*

If there were something of me you could change, I wonder
What is it you might cast aside?
Is it my pride?
Or is it the darker me inside?
Perhaps I could vie to be the man inside
of a dream you're not so eager to hide.

ICE MOUNTAINS

I was once near a frozen glacier in Alaska
and I witnessed liquid water flowing from
its core. I likened Mankind's cruelty to a
blowtorch, cutting its name into frozen
bricks of lost time and false innocence.

Craters of carelessness formed and filled
with translucent blood from the ice giant.
Geese ducked beneath shabbily constructed
bridges and started swimming in circles.
Feeling bogged down by the weight of the moment,

I began making that noise I always seem to make in the silence.
It's an audible gulp, and it starts when I swallow the lump that's
stuck in my throat. I'll pause my breath in the hopes that maybe,
just maybe, I'll be able to hear the shadow when it approaches.

Wisdom is knowing when to walk away, but, then again,
wisdom never was my strong point. So, I popped the top
off my only flare and struck it like a match. Reaching for
the steel savior I holster at the shoulder, I guided the meat of
my fingertip tightly over the trigger and began my advance.

The shadowy figure of a man was shimmering in the
crimson of the flare's light. I began wondering if he
was hiding behind the ice wall and preparing an

ambush, because he did not advance. He just stood
there, shimmering. I approached the corner with

apprehension, taking a wide-angle while
igniting my anger. I let out a roar as I raced
at the figure. He was much, much older than
I anticipated. The man in the ice was no man
at all. The man in the ice, he was neanderthal.

WITHOUT YOU

An elderly man sits in a dimly lit room pondering his loneliness as dark corners of abandonment collapse around him. Echoes from the distance are beginning their approach but from where? A place, perhaps, beyond the confines of the brick-and-mortar walls which currently safeguard his sanity.

Wiping the salted moisture of sorrow from his eyes, a merciful respite from his weeping ensues as his gaze becomes affixed to a familiar presence. Beauty and brightness dance softly, highlighting its aura and quickening its advancement through the night.

As the figure gracefully halts its advancement not three steps before him, it begins to warmly serenade his downtrodden soul through a most familiar tone of hushed laughter. In whisper, she speaks to him now.

"You must not weep so, my love."

As the celestial representation of she who he once loved so desperately begins to dissipate, a single word escapes his parched lips.

"Wait. . ."

SAVE YOUR LOVE

A kiss is just a kiss, I'm reminded. Be that ever so true, or be that ever so shrewd, the embodiment of a kiss creates something which is more than just a show of affection. Perhaps you revere a kiss as something which is intently puckered before being intensely delivered upon the lips of another. I pray that you might set aside such foolish notions; that you might flatter me as I attempt to explain the immediacy of my emotion.

As I look 'pon such tender petals, I long to be nestled just there, between carpel and sepal. Delightfully speckled, my treasure lies within your deliciously filamented anther; will you allow me the pleasure of your warmth?

Perhaps not, allow me to continue. . .

I fear the sudden and unavoidable fixation which draws me on, like a fool. I approach, separating myself from countless others who, much like me, find your fragrance unavoidable. Can you see me?

Come now, surely, you've noticed. . .

The flames within my tiny heart serve only to keep you warm as I swarm, dancing busily outside your bedroom chamber. Hold tight my love, I come for you now.

Bravely, I risk everything.

Foolishly, I fear nothing.

Dear Tiger Lily,
Save all your love,
Just for me.
Your one
Your only
Honeybee.

A GOOD MAN

A good man approaches the curiously calm waters of an oasis. Though these waters appear quite still and tranquil, they seem too good to be true. Playfully, he kicks off a single sandal and dabs at the water with the tips of his toes. Indeed, to the good man's amusement, the waters are soothing to the touch. Curiosity piques as an after-effect of sorts is revealed, warming his body from within. Lost within the moment, unknowingly, he surrenders.

"How pleasant," he whispers to himself, "I wonder—"

Should these waters be so utterly pleasing by way of a simple touch, then surely an inherent promise of pure delight would be realized if he were to choose a greater degree of immersion. So, the good man slips off his other sandal and draws a deep breath, just for luck, before stepping in with the other foot. Unbeknownst to the good man, watery fingertips grip softly around his ankles and an overflow of endorphins overwhelms receptors within his once brilliant brain. He is immediately overwhelmed by false euphoria.

As the once good man continues to wade through the forbidden waters, his body and his mind begin to betray him. Delving deeper, then deeper still, waters of false promise rapidly consume his ability to form rational thought.

Beckoned and betrayed by the devils of distillation he's become, like the Djinn of old, imprisoned within a bottle.

Notes

AUTUMN RAIN

As stated in the poem, I love the mild depression that sets in during a nice autumn rain. The cool air and earthy smells make melancholy seem magnificent. A warm drink and some family interaction make autumn rain that much more enjoyable. The rest of the poem was just me allowing my imagination to wander.

CYCLICAL

Imagining chlorophyll soldiers marching up and down the inner workings of plant life was where this poem took its original direction. I later built the front and back ends around those soldiers. Photosynthesis was used as a sort of combustion effect within the poem, resulting in a poem I fell in love with immediately. The mention of humans plucking flowers for the fragrance was a way of demonstrating how we inadvertently extract love from the world around us.

A SOULFUL SOUTHERN MORNING

I envisioned myself sitting at my mother's house and sipping morning coffee with her at the kitchen window in my hometown of Wetumpka, Alabama. I then shifted my point of view to assume that I still lived there.

My mother's love for nature and animals is something I view as an inherited trait and not just something I picked up along the way.

OF PERSIMMONS AND PLUMS

I wrestled with this poem for weeks and, at some point along the way, I actually thought the poem might have defeated me. Truth be known, the original centered around the tea and the loss of a lover, but the addition of plated plums gave me all the boost I needed. Maybe proper flavor profiles really do make a difference.

CARTRIDGE

At age 38, I had ambitions of staying in the army for another few years, but an immovable set of circumstances accompanied by a body that was falling apart at the seams made that impossible. My memory of that time served as the beginning of the poem and is a vivid representation of how I felt. The end of the poem uses the three-volley salute that is given at a service member's funeral as a sort of befitting end. The flag from atop the casket is folded with three spent cartridges neatly tucked in.

BORDERS

The opening monostich represents how I go about setting up my defenses when my depression begins getting the best of me. The chains represent how my mind goes about justifying its defenses. The monostich that brings an end to the poem shows the sense of love that I crave when I lower my defenses.

IN THE DARKNESS

I wanted to do a poem where the reader would be left to guess which of the two characters moved away from the land of the living. I wanted to make it a little scary but not so much that it lost meaning. I find myself marveling at the fact that a solid argument can be made for either of the characters.

PHOENIX

I wanted to show one of my characters searching for the meaning of life, and I wanted a friend of that character to disagree with that course of action. I also wanted the question of judging others' beliefs to be expressed because our beliefs are very personal and very important.

SKIES OF BLUE LONELINESS

There are many paths that a person may take as they deal with the symptoms of depression and there are many ways in which depression manifests itself. This poem is about my depression and my journey—chasing skies of blue loneliness.

A RIDE THROUGH THE NIGHT

I wanted to create a poem that was a unique journey through space and time. I used celestial objects in the night sky and imagined a new purpose for them. These objects are not used in any accurate or scientific method, and nothing within the work should be perceived as fact. This was one poet's attempt at creating his own mythology. Please, read on if you would like an explanation of this imaginary path:

1. The narrator's soul has been circling the earth for an entire year.
2. The narrator is released from the earth's orbit.
3. The narrator begins the ride and discovers time travel by way of folding space, this results in the narrator's near-instant arrival at the ice giant (Uranus).
4. The bright star near the feet of the hunter (Orion) is Rigel,
5. I envisioned the nebulae at the bottom of Orion as showing the narrator various reflections of mankind's journey.

6. Exiting these nebulae, the narrator is thrust into one more nebula. This time, the narrator is offered some self-reflection along with the promise that love is never-ending.

7. The beetle facing the narrator is meant to be Betelgeuse, located on what one might consider being the left shoulder of Orion (at least that's how I see it).

8. Orion claims the narrator's steed and transforms it into an arrow, whipping that arrow through the Gemini constellation (Castor and Pollux).

9. The narrator is found to be worthy, so is shot from Orion's bow.

10. In transit, the narrator catches a glimpse of the Goat Star in the Flaming Star Nebula. I wanted to show human clay being formed and the soul being attached (more of my mythology).

11. The end of the road, or perhaps the beginning, is when the narrator sets foot on cherry blossom petals (the Galactic Cherry Blossom).

DARE TO REMEMBER

This poem started with the opening monostich and a vision to discuss how loneliness could be felt by individuals in a group. I tried to imagine a therapist reflecting on previous studies of loneliness. The rain gauge experiment was an invention of mine that I found very thought-provoking. I view the idea of frolicking in the rain as inviting the rain to play (the opposite of loneliness). Lastly, don't forget to remember how important you are. Remember—you.

CICADAS AND SYCAMORES

Sycamore trees and cicadas are both found throughout Oklahoma and are both beautiful (as is the rest of nature). The story behind the poem was centered around the memories of one character. I wanted the poem to be built from childhood memories, and I wanted it to end with an adult's perspective.

MY CURSE

This was one of those poems that sat in a folder on my hard drive waiting for the right words. I truly am one of those people who has a history of failure when it comes to expressing emotions. Maybe that's why I tend to write so many romantic poems.

NEVER BEEN HERE BEFORE

As the poem reads, I have often heard of love being expressed as a who or a what, but never a where. So, where is love? I used the iris flower as a visual because of the iris in the eye (of course) and because of the wide array of colors that the iris comes in.

NOTHING LEFT TO SAY

Believe it or not, this poem is about a family's struggle with addiction. Addiction takes many forms and is not just about the consumption of alcohol, chemicals, or medications. Life is not without obstacles, but we do the best we can. Here, the narrator only wants to know if their loved one is safe.

RED FROM ROSES

I had the first stanza of this poem stuck in a different poem; I cannot remember which. I thought the stanza was beautiful and that it just had to begin its very own poem

About the five perceived centuries of loneliness: 365 (days in a standard year) x 100 (a century) x 5 (5 centuries) ÷ 24 (hours in a day) ÷ 60 (Minutes in a day) ÷ 60 (seconds in a minute) = 2+days. The narrator felt so in love that 2 days apart seemed like five centuries and was rewarded a rose per actual day as a sort of compensation.

BEAUTIFUL

This was my first attempt at writing an acrostic poem. I edited it over and over again until it turned out right. The first thing I wanted was for the poem to live up to its title; it had to be a beautiful read. Then, I just wanted a love poem with seamless transitions.

MY FATHER'S SON

I lost my biological father when I was very young. My stepfather gave the children in our household a glowing example of manhood. As the years passed and three boys became men, he'd earned every bit of the name "father."

He and my mother showed all of us how a loving couple could make a marriage last.

This poem is about my mother's husband—this poem is about my dad.

A DOG

I was diagnosed with cancer just two years after retiring from the military. My emotions were a mess, and I cannot tell you how difficult it was to smile, but Louie (my dog) changed all of that. He was the perfect dog at the perfect time.

WAKING UP

This is the day you realize that the clock caught up by a few clicks, the moment when you realize that you just might have to be a little more careful than you'd been just the day before.

CHIN-WHISKERS

Just in case you haven't seen or read about it yet, I am a retired soldier. Most of that tough guy business went out of the window when my granddaughter was born. The rest was gone when my great-granddaughter was born. I do not want to be a tough guy anymore; I just want to be there.

COLD BURNING COAL

The premise behind this poem was centered around a man who stole a kiss from his love interest. He suffers from regret over his actions (perhaps judging himself too harshly). His heart has grown cold, but it does not stop beating due to an infusion of cold burning coal, something I view as a force within him that works alongside old man winter to convince him of his worthiness of a second chance.

ICE COLD FUSION

My second attempt at an acrostic poem. While not as long or complex as the other poem (Beautiful), I do love the whole thought around Ice cold Fusion.

DREAMS

My wife and I tease each other over which of us was the hunter when first we met. As the old-fashioned male in our relationship, I see myself as the protector. As a man who has experienced a couple of run-ins with illness, I have also been the protected. Perspective!

HIGH ON A ROOFTOP

This poem began with the opening line. From there the poem just kind of built itself into an "all in the day of" kind of piece. I like to insert a long pause in the final stanza when reading it aloud, just to see if anyone thinks the man on the ledge has other intentions (he does not because harming oneself should not be an answer).

A DAY SOAKING IN SUNSHINE

Louie (my dog) and I went outside together many times over the years. On one occasion, I took my journal with me and sat with the sun on my back. I watched Louie embrace the world around him and just wrote. That day was a true gift, and I am so happy to be able to share it with you.

A COOL SPRING DAY AT THE ZOO

My wife thought I was crazy for bringing a notebook into the zoo this year, but joy and beauty are where you find them, and I wanted to capture our day at the zoo in words. The primates were really enjoying those blankets and, yes, the zookeeper said the elephant was geriatric and her favorite snacks were onions (she ate quite a few as we watched). I have always loved the zoo.

TAKE MY HAND

Another love poem (sorry, I'm a romantic). It is a conventional love story about a man and a woman and about how they are blessed with a family. If the poem does not fit your reality, a little bit of imagination should do the trick.

FEELS LIKE ZEN

I do not consider myself an expert on anything Zen, but I do feel as though there is a lot to be learned when we choose to open our minds. To be honest, this poem shows my journey as I wonder about how I fit into the world around me.

CRYING

I sat on the opening line "Today, I saw the clouds cry" for months. Every single time I tried to make it work, I failed. One day, when looking for something I wanted to read for the monthly open mic night, I threw caution to the wind and started pecking away at the keyboard. I hope you like it.

TELL ME

I'm a sucker for unique rhyme schemes and it is my opinion that this poem has just that. Each stanza is enveloped and filled with love (and rhyme).

THROUGH YOUR EYES

I wrote the first version of this poem in a poetry class, and I hated it. Others seemed to like it, so I dressed it up a little and added the third stanza and moved the stanzas around. It's an interesting poem because people either love it or hate it. Depending on how I feel on a certain day, I love it or hate it.

ICE MOUNTAINS

I never thought we'd reach a point, at least in my lifetime, where so many of our glaciers were melting so rapidly. It would be ideal if our planet's glaciers were allowed to keep their secrets, but if they cannot, I wonder what we'll find.

WITHOUT YOU

This was originally written to be a 100-word micro-fiction story. I dressed it up with some assonance and alliteration, resulting in a poem that I refer to as being *tragically beautiful.*

SAVE YOUR LOVE

I am a gardener who loves to see the honeybees out and about. I do not, however, plant tiger lilies. This is because my dog eats dirt, and lilies can be toxic to the little guy.

A GOOD MAN

This poem is about alcoholism and about how easy it is for some of us to go from a few drinks to a few drinks too far. It is not meant to pass judgment in any way, shape, or form.